Take 5

QUILTS FROM JUST 5 FABRICS

· ·

Kathy Brown

Martingale®
& COMPANY

Take 5: Quilts From Just 5 Fabrics
© 2010 by Kathy Brown

That Patchwork Place® is an imprint of Martingale & Company®.

Martingale & Company
19021 120th Ave. NE, Suite 102
Bothell, WA 98011-9511 USA
www.martingale-pub.com

Printed in China
15 14 13 12   8 7 6 5

Library of Congress Cataloging-in-Publication Data is available upon request.

ISBN: 978-1-56477-909-0

Mission Statement

Dedicated to providing quality products and service to inspire creativity.

Credits

President & CEO • Tom Wierzbicki
Editor in Chief • Mary V. Green
Managing Editor • Tina Cook
Developmental Editor • Karen Costello Soltys
Technical Editor • Laurie Baker
Copy Editor • Melissa Bryan
Design Director • Stan Green
Production Manager • Regina Girard
Illustrator • Laurel Strand
Cover & Text Designer • Adrienne Smitke
Photographer • Brent Kane

Contents

The Take 5 Technique

I've always been a firm believer that good things come from humble beginnings. I became aware of quilting at an early age when I would go to sleepovers at my great-aunt's home, which lay in the shadows of Ashland-Belle Helene Plantation in southeastern Louisiana. Nanny, as we affectionately called her, had a Civil War–era bed in the hall bedroom. The mattress was situated high so that the balmy Southern night air could pass under and around the bed to keep you cool in the summertime. In the winter, we were comforted at night with quilts, lovingly placed one by one on top of us until we were burrowed beneath like little mice. Nanny made all the quilts by hand, cutting the pieces from clothes long discarded and feed sacks that had held the grains and food staples used in the home and for the farm animals. She quilted them with loving care on a frame made by my great-uncle. These quilts, simple and functional, had their roots in modest beginnings. As I have journeyed into the world of quilting, it has been these simple and humble aspects of life that have formed my foundation as a quiltmaker.

Several years ago, good fortune came my way when a new quilt shop opened up just a couple of miles from my home. The owners and I quickly became friends, and I spent a great deal of time helping out there at the Quilt Corner. This offered me numerous opportunities to assist customers in choosing their fabrics. What I noticed time and time again was that when a quilt required a lot of fabrics, the customer often became flustered and overwhelmed with the fabric-choosing process. The more fabric that was required, the worse the frustration became. In my heart, I knew there just had to be a better way, a more simplistic and stress-free approach to this process. I was sure that scrappy-looking quilts could be achieved without having to coordinate large amounts of fabric. From those thoughts, my Take 5 technique evolved.

The Take 5 technique works on the premise of five simple concepts:

1. Use five fabrics to create simply stunning quilts.
2. Take five minutes to choose these five fabrics.
3. Stack the fabrics and cut out the pieces simultaneously.
4. Take your cuts and organize them into groups prior to sewing.
5. Relax and have fun!

First, start with your focus fabric. This is the fabric that you absolutely fall in love with, have to have, can't live without—you know the one! Take that fabric, and from there, choose four fabrics in colors that are present in the focus fabric. Look for variety among the four fabrics. For example, if you started with a large-scale floral fabric for the focus piece, consider adding a small-scale tone-on-tone floral, a plaid or stripe, a small dot print, and another interesting print that will add to the variety and color in your mix of fabrics.

This process of choosing the four supporting fabrics shouldn't take any longer than five minutes or so. If you take much longer, you'll start to question your decisions, the frustration will set in, and you'll be back to square one. Having used this process literally hundreds of times at quilt shops and with quilt guilds, one characteristic always stands out: if a quilter spends more than 10 minutes choosing her fabrics, and she waffles back and forth between fabrics before finally making her ultimate selection, 90% of the time the quilter

*Choose your focus fabric (on the bottom in these two groupings),
and then select four additional fabrics to go with it.*

returns to the first five fabrics she started with. Why? Because our gut instinct tells us what we like—our eyes tell us immediately what's pleasing. Those are the fabrics we liked in the beginning, and they're the ones that we really want.

When you take longer to choose your fabrics, your brain and emotions generally make you start questioning your choices. You may ask the sales associate if your choices are "OK," or turn to your friends to see what they like, rather than trusting your initial impulses. Ultimately, if you rely on the help of others to choose your fabrics, you may go home with fabrics that don't even truly appeal to you, and you'll end up making a quilt that's not really yours. Keep it simple, go with your instincts, and you'll be happy.

Once all five fabrics have been selected, you'll need to decide which two you'll use for the inner and outer borders, and then purchase more yardage for those fabrics. The border fabrics are typically your two favorites out of the grouping—usually the focus fabric and one other—but this certainly doesn't have to be the case. Once you've decided

on the fabrics for the borders, the fabric-choosing process is over—and ideally it took just five minutes or so! (Please note that in a couple of the projects in this book I've added a "neutral" fabric that the other fabrics would work with, such as a white fabric or muslin.)

The next step in the Take 5 technique involves stacking your fabrics and cutting them simultaneously, which is a huge time-saving aspect of the technique. After all your pieces are cut, you organize them into groups. This step is so very important because it completely takes the guesswork out of what to do next. Your fabrics are cut and organized, and the sewing can begin!

The Take 5 technique works because it is simple, regardless of the design and how complicated a project *may* look. It gives you a foundation to start from (your focus fabric), and you build from that point. You'll have fun, and you'll complete more quilts in less time than you ever thought possible.

Quiltmaking Basics

Successful Take 5 quilts require a few basic supplies and simple instructions. Follow the guidelines in this section as you construct your quilts.

Materials

You don't need any fancy tools and supplies to make a Take 5 quilt. If you've done any amount of quilting, you probably have most of these items on hand.

- Good-quality, 100%-cotton fabrics
- Neutral-colored thread
- Rotary cutter
- 24" x 36" rotary-cutting mat
- 8½" x 24½" acrylic rotary-cutting ruler
- Self-adhesive grip tabs (to keep your rulers from slipping)
- Glass-head pins
- Seam ripper
- Sewing machine in good working order with a ¼" presser foot
- Hand embroidery needles

Rotary Cutting

Because rotary cutting is a topic covered in so many quilting books, I won't go into great detail here on how to use a rotary cutter. What you do need to remember as you begin each new project in this book is to start with a new rotary-cutter blade. You will be cutting through multiple layers of fabric and will need the sharp, accurate edge that a new blade provides.

1. Open each cut of fabric and press the center fold. I prefer to starch the fabrics at this time so that I get a more accurate cut, but this is a personal preference.
2. With the fabrics still open, lay the fabrics down on your cutting mat, one on top of the other, with the selvages to your left and right. Lay your 8½" x 24½" ruler over the left edge. Check to make sure that all the layers of fabric are showing underneath the ruler and that you will be trimming off all of the selvages. Using your rotary cutter, cut along the right edge of the ruler. Slide the ruler upward as you come to the end of it, keeping the edge of the ruler aligned with the cut edge of the fabric. Discard the selvages.

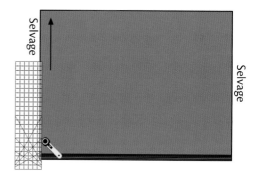

3. Rotate the fabric or reposition your body so that the newly cut edge is closest to you. Align the short end of the ruler with the straightened edge of the fabric stack in the same manner as you cut the selvage edges, and trim off the raw edges on the left side.

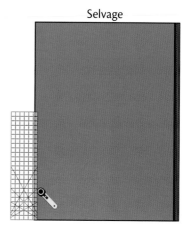

4. Having made the edges square, you're ready to begin cutting your fabrics. Follow the cutting guides included in each quilt project to make the individual cuts. Refer to steps 2 and 3 to restraighten the edges after you've made several cuts or if the layers shift while cutting.

Pinning and Pressing

To pin or not to pin—this is a decision that most quilters face somewhere along their quilting journey. I've found, through much trial, error, and angst, that it's far better to take the time to pin. Your piecing will be more accurate and you'll spend less time ripping out seams when the pieces don't fit together properly. If you choose not to pin, that's your personal choice, but don't say I didn't urge you to do so!

Accurate pressing is also a must in my opinion. As with pinning, I find that my blocks fit together better and are much straighter if I press each seam after sewing it.

Adding Borders

All the quilts in this book feature borders with butted corners. Cut border strips across the width of the fabric, and then piece them together when necessary to achieve the required length.

To piece border strips, place the ends of the strips right sides together, and then sew diagonally from the point where the strips meet at the top of the horizontal strip to the point where the strips meet at the bottom of the horizontal strip. Trim ¼" from the stitching line and press the seam allowances open.

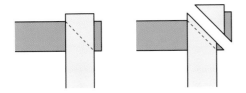

To add the borders to the quilt, mark the center point of each edge of the quilt top. Mark the center point on one long edge of each border strip. With right sides together, pin the side border strips to the quilt top, matching the center marks. There will be excess border fabric extending beyond the quilt-top edges. Stitch the borders in place, and then trim the excess border-strip fabric even with the top and bottom edges. Press the seam allowances toward the border strips. Repeat for the top and bottom borders, trimming the excess even with the sides of the quilt top.

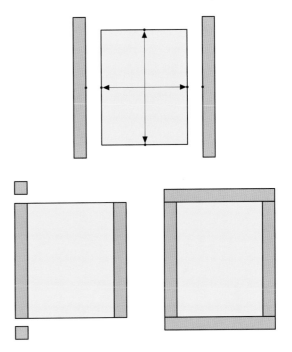

Completing the Quilt

There are just a few more things to do before your quilt is finished.

LAYERING AND QUILTING

Before the quilting begins, you need to make sure that your backing and batting are at least 4" wider and longer than the quilt top. The material requirements listed in each project have allowed for this excess. Layer the batting between the backing and the quilt top, and quilt as desired.

All quilts in this book were quilted on long-arm quilting machines, but you can certainly use any quilting method that you prefer.

BINDING

The quilts shown in this book were bound using the traditional double-fold method. Yardage indicated for the binding of each quilt, with the exception of "Take 5 . . . Across the Miles" (page 31), is for strips cut 2½" wide. Cut strips across the width of the fabric and join them with a diagonal seam in the same manner as for border strips (see page 7) to make one long strip.

1. Press the binding strip in half lengthwise, wrong sides together.
2. Leaving an 8" to 10" tail at the beginning, sew the binding to the quilt top using a ¼" seam allowance. Miter the corners as shown.

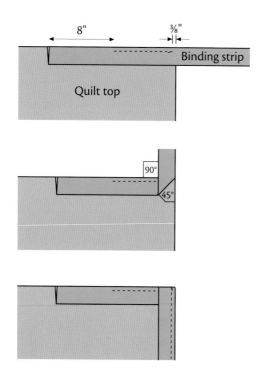

3. Stop sewing when you are about 12" from the beginning; backstitch. Overlap the end of the strip with the beginning of the strip that you left unstitched. Trim the end of the binding strip so that it overlaps the same amount as the width of the binding strip (2½" for all the quilts except

"Take 5 . . . Across the Miles"). Sew the two ends together as shown and trim, leaving a ¼" seam allowance. Press the seam allowances open. Reposition the binding on the quilt and finish sewing.

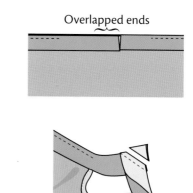

4. Fold the edge of the binding to the back of the quilt and hand stitch it in place, mitering the corners. I find that the binding folds over the edge more easily if I apply spray starch to it at this point, and then press it toward the sewn edge.

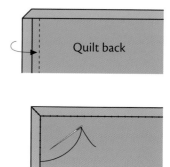

Take 5... Takes a Walk around the Block

Rectangles take a walk around squares as the fabrics change position from block to block in this fun-to-construct quilt.

Finished Quilt: 64" x 76"
Finished Block: 12" x 12"

Materials

Yardage is based on 42"-wide fabric.
⅝ yard of cream floral for blocks
⅝ yard of gold striped fabric for blocks
⅝ yard of black floral for blocks
⅝ yard of green leaf print for blocks
⅝ yard of rust print for blocks
⅔ yard of one of the block fabrics for inner border
2¼ yards of one of the block fabrics for outer border and binding
4⅔ yards of fabric for backing
72" x 84" piece of batting

Cutting the Layered Pieces

Refer to "Rotary Cutting" on page 6 to stack the fabrics on top of each other and straighten the edges. Refer to the cutting diagram below to cut the layered fabrics into the following pieces, cutting in order from left to right.

From *each* of the ⅝-yard cuts of fabric for blocks, cut:
4 squares, 8½" x 8½" (20 total)
8 rectangles, 2½" x 8½" (40 total)
8 rectangles, 2½" x 12½" (40 total)

Cutting the Remaining Pieces

From the fabric for inner border, cut:
8 strips, 2½" x 42"

From the fabric for outer border and binding, cut:
8 strips, 6½" x 42"
8 strips, 2½" x 42"

Designed and quilted by Kathy Brown; pieced by Linda Reed

Constructing the Blocks

1. Organize the layered block pieces into stacks, separating them first by fabric and then by size. Label the fabrics 1–5.

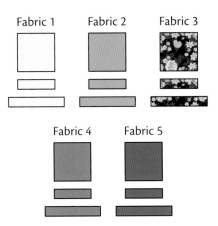

2. To make block A, sew a 2½" x 8½" rectangle of fabric 3 to the top edge of a fabric 1 square and a 2½" x 8½" rectangle of fabric 5 to the bottom edge of the square as shown. Press the seam allowances toward the rectangles. Add a 2½" x 12½" rectangle of fabric 4 to the left side of this unit and a 2½" x 12½" rectangle of fabric 2 to the right side of this unit. Repeat to make a total of four blocks.

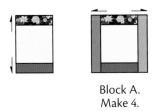

Block A.
Make 4.

3. Repeat step 2 with the remaining squares and rectangles in the combinations shown to make blocks B–E. Make four of each block.

Block B.   Block C.   Block D.   Block E.
Make 4.   Make 4.   Make 4.   Make 4.

Assembling the Quilt Top

1. Refer to the quilt assembly diagram to arrange the blocks into five rows of four blocks each, using a design wall or other flat surface.
2. Sew the blocks in each row together. Press the seam allowances in opposite directions from row to row. Sew the rows together. Press the seam allowances in one direction.

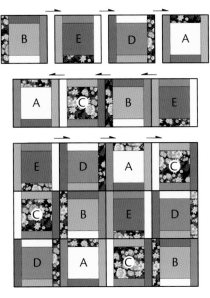

Quilt assembly

Adding the Borders

1. Referring to "Adding Borders" on page 7, join two 2½" x 42" inner-border strips end to end to make one long strip. Repeat to make a total of four pieced strips. Sew the border strips to the quilt top. Press.
2. Repeat step 1 to add the 6½" x 42" outer-border strips to the quilt top.

Finishing

Refer to "Completing the Quilt" on page 7 to layer the quilt top, batting, and backing. Quilt as desired. Bind the quilt with the 2½"-wide binding strips.

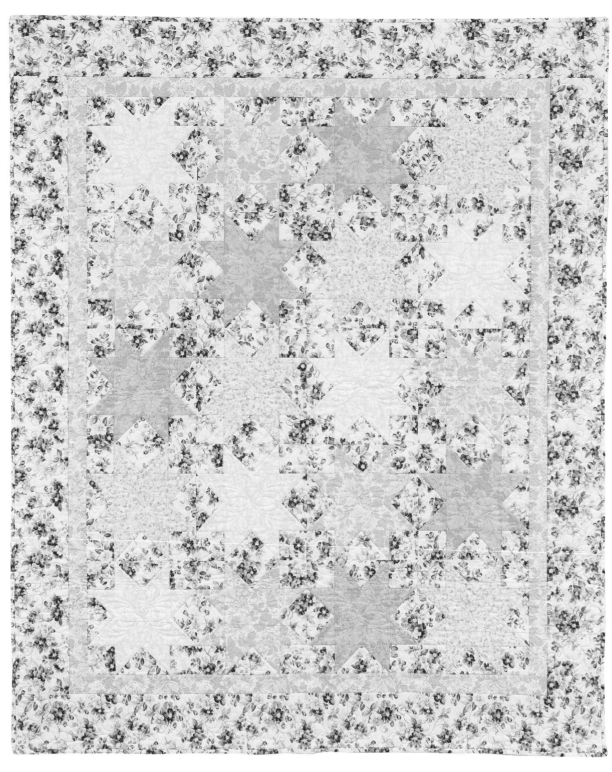

Designed by Kathy Brown; pieced by Pam Vierra McGinnis; quilted by Carol Hilton

Take 5... Reaches for the Stars

Subtle floral fabrics blend in perfect harmony to create this soft, romantic star quilt.

. . . .

Finished Quilt: 64" x 76"
Finished Block: 12" x 12"

. . . .

Materials

Yardage is based on 42"-wide fabric.

¾ yard of pale blue floral tone-on-tone fabric for blocks

¾ yard of pale pink floral tone-on-tone fabric for blocks

¾ yard of pale green floral tone-on-tone fabric for blocks

¾ yard of pale tan floral tone-on-tone fabric for blocks

4⅜ yards of cream floral for blocks, outer border, and binding

⅔ yard of one of the pale tone-on-tone block fabrics for inner border

4⅔ yards of fabric for backing

72" x 84" piece of batting

Cutting the Layered Pieces

Refer to "Rotary Cutting" on page 6 to stack the fabrics on top of each other and straighten the edges. Refer to the cutting diagram below to cut the layered fabrics into the following pieces, cutting pieces of the same size in order from left to right.

From *each* of the ¾-yard cuts of fabric for blocks, cut:
5 squares, 6½" x 6½" (20 total)
40 squares, 3½" x 3½" (160 total)

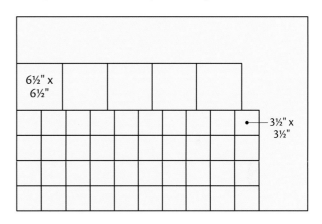

Cutting the Remaining Pieces

From the cream floral, cut:
21 strips, 3½" x 42"; crosscut into:
       80 squares, 3½" x 3½"
       80 rectangles, 3½" x 6½"
8 strips, 6½" x 42"
8 strips, 2½" x 42"

From the fabric for inner border, cut:
8 strips, 2½" x 42"

Constructing the Blocks

1. Organize the layered block pieces and the cream floral squares and rectangles into stacks, separating them first by fabric and then by size. Label the fabrics 1–5, with the cream floral squares and rectangles as fabric 5.

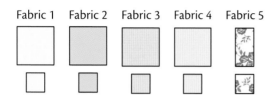

Fabric 1   Fabric 2   Fabric 3   Fabric 4   Fabric 5

2. With a fabric-marking pencil, draw a diagonal line from corner to corner on the wrong side of each 3½" square of fabrics 1–4.

3. To make block A, with right sides together and raw edges aligned, position a 3½" square of fabric 1 on the left end of a fabric 5 rectangle, orienting the marked line as shown. Sew on the marked line. Trim ¼" from the stitching line. Press back the resulting triangle. Repeat on the right end of the rectangle. Repeat to make a total of 20 identical flying-geese units.

Make 20.

4. Sew flying-geese units to opposite sides of a 6½" fabric 1 square as shown. Press the seam allowances toward the square. Repeat to make a total of five units.

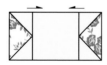

Make 5.

5. Sew a 3½" square of fabric 5 to each end of the remaining flying-geese units. Press the seam allowances toward the squares.

Make 10.

6. Join the units from step 5 to the top and bottom edges of the units from step 4. Press the seam allowances toward the top and bottom rows.

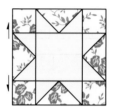

Block A.
Make 5.

7. Repeat steps 3–6 with the remaining block pieces in the combinations shown to make blocks B–D. Make five of each block.

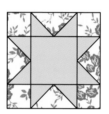 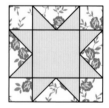

Block B.   Block C.
Make 5.   Make 5.

Block D.
Make 5.

Assembling the Quilt Top

1. Refer to the quilt assembly diagram to arrange the blocks into five rows of four blocks each, using a design wall or other flat surface.
2. Sew the blocks in each row together. Press the seam allowances in opposite directions from row to row. Sew the rows together. Press the seam allowances in one direction.

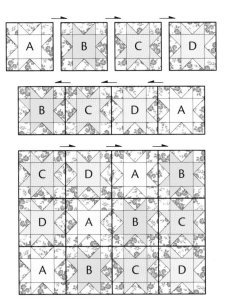

Quilt assembly

Adding the Borders

1. Referring to "Adding Borders" on page 7, join two 2½" x 42" inner-border strips end to end to make one long strip. Repeat to make a total of four pieced strips. Sew the border strips to the quilt top. Press.
2. Repeat step 1 to add the cream floral 6½"-wide outer-border strips to the quilt top.

Finishing

Refer to "Completing the Quilt" on page 7 to layer the quilt top, batting, and backing. Quilt as desired. Bind the quilt with the cream floral 2½"-wide strips.

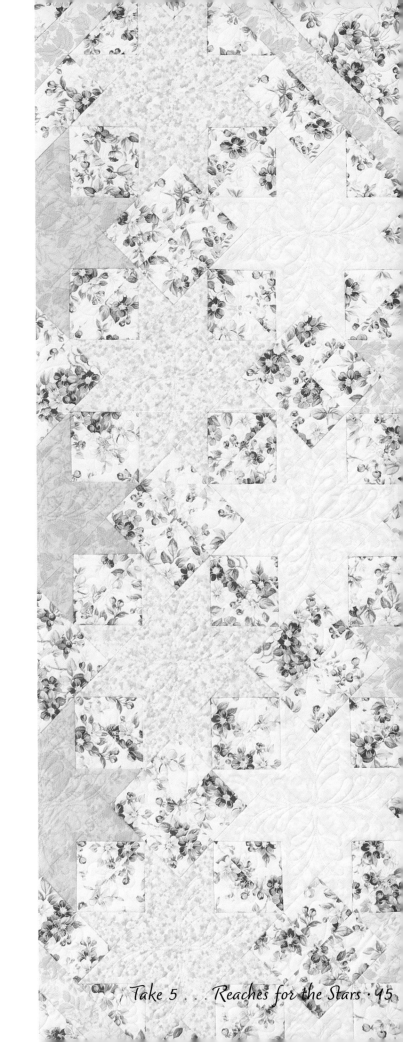

Designed by Kathy Brown; pieced by Linda Reed; quilted by Carol Hilton

Take 5...Turns over a New Leaf

Rich autumn batiks come together to create a warm and inviting lap quilt.

Finished Quilt: 64" x 76"
Finished Block: 12" x 12"

Materials

Yardage is based on 42"-wide fabric.
1 yard of multicolored batik for blocks
1 yard of deep brown batik for blocks
1 yard of orange batik for blocks
1 yard of light green batik for blocks
1 yard of deep flame red batik for blocks
⅔ yard of one of the block batiks for inner border
2¼ yards of one of the block batiks for outer border and binding
4⅔ yards of fabric for backing
72" x 84" piece of batting

Cutting the Layered Pieces

Refer to "Rotary Cutting" on page 6 to stack the fabrics on top of each other and straighten the edges. Refer to the cutting diagram below to cut the layered fabrics into the following pieces, cutting in order from left to right.

From *each* of the 1-yard cuts of fabric for blocks, cut:
4 rectangles, 4½" x 12½" (20 total)
4 rectangles, 4½" x 8½" (20 total)
16 squares, 4½" x 4½" (80 total)
8 squares, 4⅞" x 4⅞" (40 total)

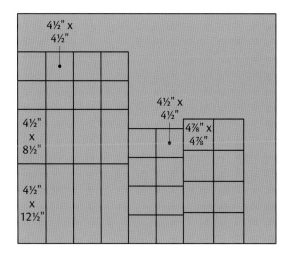

Cutting the Remaining Pieces

From the remainder of the 1-yard cuts, cut a *total* of:
20 rectangles, ¾" x 6"

From the fabric for inner border, cut:
8 strips, 2½" x 42"

From the fabric for outer border and binding, cut:
8 strips, 6½" x 42"
8 strips, 2½" x 42"

Constructing the Blocks

1. Organize the layered block pieces into stacks, separating them first by fabric and then by size. Label the fabrics 1–5.

Fabric 1	Fabric 2	Fabric 3	Fabric 4	Fabric 5

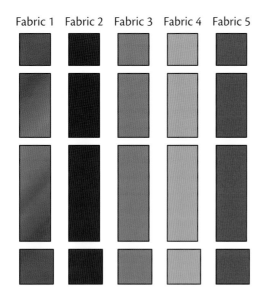

2. To make block A, use a fabric-marking pencil to draw a diagonal line from corner to corner on the wrong side of 8 of the 4½" squares of fabric 3.

3. With right sides together and raw edges aligned, position a marked fabric 3 square at the top of a 4½" x 8½" fabric 2 rectangle, orienting the marked line as shown. Stitch on the marked line. Trim ¼" from the stitching line. Press back the resulting triangle. Repeat to make a total of four units.

Make 4.

4. Select a ¾" x 6" rectangle that will show up well as a stem on fabric 3. Press the long raw edges ¼" to the wrong side. With the raw edges face down, lay the wrong side of the strip diagonally across the right side of an unmarked 4½" fabric 3 square so that the ends of the strip extend beyond

the corners. Stitch the strip in place ⅛" from the long edges. Repeat to make a total of four units.

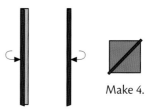

Make 4.

5. Sew a stem unit from step 4 to the bottom edge of a unit from step 3. Trim away the excess stem at the corners. Press the seam allowances toward the unit from step 3. Repeat to make a total of four units.

Make 4.

6. Repeat step 3 with the remaining marked 4½" fabric 3 squares and the 4½" x 12½" fabric 2 rectangles.

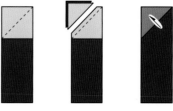

Make 4.

7. With a fabric-marking pencil, draw a diagonal line from corner to corner on the wrong side of four 4⅞" fabric 3 squares. With right sides together, position a marked square on a 4⅞" square of fabric 2, aligning the raw edges. Stitch ¼" from both sides of the marked line. Cut the squares apart on the marked line. Press the seam allowances toward fabric 2. Repeat with the remaining marked fabric

3 squares to make a total of eight half-square-triangle units.

Make 8.

8. Join two half-square-triangle units and an unmarked 4½" square of fabric 3.

9. Join one unit each from steps 5, 6, and 8 to complete the block. Repeat to make a total of four blocks.

 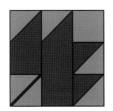

Block A.
Make 4.

10. Repeat steps 2–9 in the combinations shown to make blocks B–E. Make four of each block.

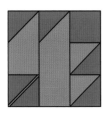 

Block B.
Make 4.

Block C.
Make 4.

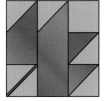 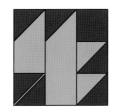

Block D.
Make 4.

Block E.
Make 4.

Assembling the Quilt Top

1. Refer to the quilt assembly diagram to arrange the blocks into five rows of four blocks each, using a design wall or other flat surface.
2. Sew the blocks in each row together. Press the seam allowances in opposite directions from row to row. Sew the rows together. Press the seam allowances in one direction.

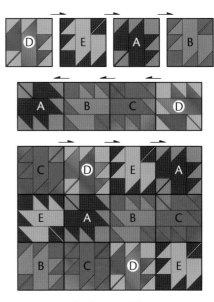

Quilt assembly

Adding the Borders

1. Referring to "Adding Borders" on page 7, join two 2½" x 42" inner-border strips end to end to make one long strip. Repeat to make a total of four pieced strips. Sew the border strips to the quilt top. Press.
2. Repeat step 1 to add the 6½" x 42" outer-border strips to the quilt top.

Finishing

Refer to "Completing the Quilt" on page 7 to layer the quilt top, batting, and backing. Quilt as desired. Bind the quilt with the 2½"-wide binding strips.

Designed by Kathy Brown; pieced by Linda Reed; quilted by Karen McTavish

Take 5...Plays Fair and Square

A square-within-a-square setting comes alive with the addition of the Take 5 technique!

Finished Quilt: 52" x 61"
Finished Block: 9" x 9"

Materials

Yardage is based on 42"-wide fabric.

¾ yard of brick red hand-dyed fabric for blocks

¾ yard of mustard hand-dyed fabric for blocks

¾ yard of olive hand-dyed fabric for blocks

¾ yard of black hand-dyed fabric for blocks

¾ yard of tan hand-dyed fabric for blocks

⅔ yard of one of the block fabrics for inner border

2⅛ yards of one of the block fabrics for outer border

3½ yards of fabric for backing

60" x 69" piece of batting

Cutting the Layered Pieces

Refer to "Rotary Cutting" on page 6 to stack the fabrics on top of each other and straighten the edges. Refer to the cutting diagram below to cut the layered fabrics into the following pieces, cutting pieces of the same size in order from left to right.

From *each* of the ¾-yard cuts of fabric for blocks, cut:
4 squares, 9½" x 9½" (20 total)
16 squares, 5" x 5" (80 total)

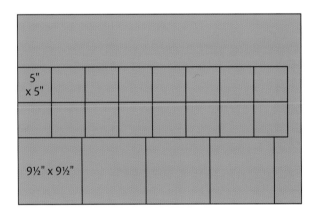

Cutting the Remaining Pieces

From the fabric for inner border, cut:
8 strips, 2½" x 42"

From the fabric for outer border, cut:
8 strips, 6½" x 42"
6 strips, 2½" x 42"

Constructing the Blocks

1. Organize the layered block pieces into stacks, separating them first by fabric and then by size. Label the fabrics 1–5.

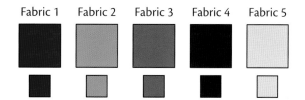

Fabric 1 Fabric 2 Fabric 3 Fabric 4 Fabric 5

2. With a fabric-marking pencil, draw a diagonal line from corner to corner on the wrong side of each 5" square.

3. To make block A, with right sides together and raw edges aligned, position a marked fabric 2 square in the upper-left corner of a 9½" square of fabric 1, orienting the marked line as shown. Sew on the marked line. Trim ¼" from the stitching line. Press back the resulting triangle. Repeat on the remaining three corners of the large square, orienting the marked lines as shown. Repeat to make a total of four blocks.

Block A.
Make 4.

4. Repeat step 3 with the remaining squares in the combinations shown to make blocks B–E. Make four of each block.

Block B.   Block C.   Block D.   Block E.
Make 4.   Make 4.   Make 4.   Make 4.

Assembling the Quilt Top

1. Refer to the quilt assembly diagram to arrange the blocks into five rows of four blocks each, using a design wall or other flat surface.

2. Sew the blocks in each row together. Press the seam allowances in opposite directions from row to row. Sew the rows together. Press the seam allowances in one direction.

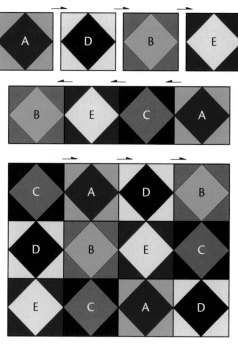

Quilt assembly

Adding the Borders

1. Referring to "Adding Borders" on page 7, join two 2½" x 42" inner-border strips end to end to make one long strip. Repeat to make a total of four pieced strips. Sew the border strips to the quilt top. Press.

2. Repeat step 1 to add the 6½" x 42" outer-border strips to the quilt top.

Finishing

Refer to "Completing the Quilt" on page 7 to layer the quilt top, batting, and backing. Quilt as desired. Bind the quilt with the 2½"-wide binding strips.

Take 5...Makes New Friends

Bright and cheerful, this fun-filled Take 5 quilt is sure to please children of all ages!

Finished Quilt: 57" x 75"
Finished Block: 9" x 9"

Materials

Yardage is based on 42"-wide fabric.
⅝ yard of bright pink mottled print for blocks
⅝ yard of bright yellow mottled print for blocks
⅝ yard of bright turquoise mottled print for blocks
⅝ yard of bright lime green mottled print for blocks
3⅛ yards of multicolored dot print for blocks, outer border, and binding
¼ yard of bright pink mottled print for inner border
¼ yard of bright lime green mottled print for inner border
¼ yard of bright turquoise mottled print for inner border
¼ yard of bright yellow mottled print for inner border
4⅝ yards of fabric for backing
65" x 83" piece of batting

Cutting the Layered Pieces

Refer to "Rotary Cutting" on page 6 to stack the fabrics on top of each other and straighten the edges. Refer to the cutting diagram below to cut the layered fabrics into the following pieces, cutting in order from left to right.

From *each* of the ⅝-yard cuts of fabric for blocks, cut:
5 squares, 9½" x 9½" (20 total; you will use 18)
9 squares, 3⅞" x 3⅞" (36 total)

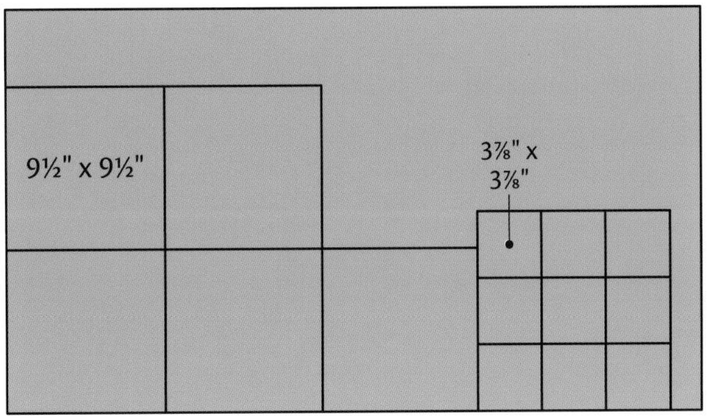

9½" x 9½"		3⅞" x 3⅞"

Cutting the Remaining Pieces

From the multicolored dot print, cut:
8 strips, 3½" x 42"; crosscut into 85 squares, 3½" x 3½"
4 strips, 3⅞" x 42"; crosscut into 36 squares, 3⅞" x 3⅞"
8 strips, 5" x 42"
7 strips, 2½" x 42"

From *each* of the ¼-yard cuts of bright mottled print, cut:
2 strips, 2" x 42" (8 total)

Designed by Kathy Brown; pieced by Linda Reed; quilted by Ellen Rushin

Constructing the Blocks

1. Organize the layered block pieces and the multicolored dot squares into stacks, separating them first by fabric and then by size. Label the fabrics 1–5, with the multicolored dot squares as fabric 5.

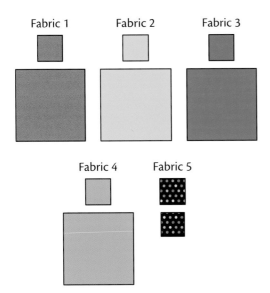

Fabric 1   Fabric 2   Fabric 3

Fabric 4   Fabric 5

2. With a fabric-marking pencil, draw a diagonal line from corner to corner on the wrong side of each bright mottled print 3⅞" square. With right sides together, position a marked square on a 3⅞" square of fabric 5, aligning the raw edges. Stitch ¼" from both sides of the marked line. Cut the squares apart on the marked line. Press the seam allowances toward fabric 5. Repeat with the remaining marked squares to make 18 half-square-triangle units of each color (72 total). Discard one unit of each color.

Make 18
of each color.
Discard one
of each color.

3. Arrange one half-square-triangle unit of each color and five 3½" squares of fabric 5 into three horizontal rows. Be sure that the half-square-triangle units are oriented

as shown to form the design and that the colors are in the correct position. Sew the pieces in each row together. Press the seam allowances toward the fabric 5 squares. Sew the rows together. Press the seam allowances away from the middle row. Repeat to make a total of 17 blocks.

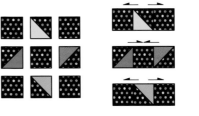

Make 17.

Assembling the Quilt Top

1. Refer to the quilt assembly diagram to arrange the blocks and bright mottled print 9½" squares into seven rows, alternating the blocks and squares within each row and from row to row.

2. Sew the blocks in each row together. Press the seam allowances toward the bright mottled print squares. Sew the rows together. Press the seam allowances in one direction.

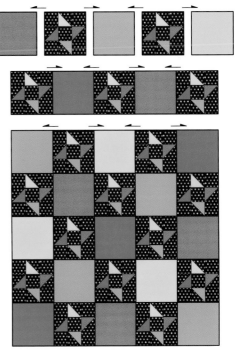

Quilt assembly

Adding the Borders

1. Referring to "Adding Borders" on page 7, join the two lime green 2" x 42" inner-border strips end to end to make one long strip. Repeat with the remaining pairs of mottled print strips. Sew the border strips to the quilt top, referring to the photo on page 24 for color placement or adding them in the order desired.
2. Join two multicolored dot print 5" x 42" outer-border strips together end to end to make one long strip. Repeat to make a total of four pieced strips. Add the border strips to the quilt top.

Finishing

Refer to "Completing the Quilt" on page 7 to layer the quilt top, batting, and backing. Quilt as desired. Bind the quilt with the multicolored dot print 2½"-wide strips.

Take 5...Crosses the Line

Fresh as a spring day, a cool blend of blue and green prints gets an added boost from a white backdrop in this ever-so-easy Take 5 quilt.

Finished Quilt: 64¾" x 81"
Finished Block: 11½" x 11½"

Materials

Yardage is based on 42"-wide fabric.
⅝ yard of blue floral for blocks
⅝ yard of multicolored print for blocks
⅝ yard of blue-on-green print for blocks
⅝ yard of green-on-blue print for blocks
⅝ yard of green-on-white print for blocks
2⅛ yards of white tone-on-tone print for blocks and setting triangles
⅔ yard of one of the block prints for inner border
2¼ yards of one of the block prints for outer border and binding
5 yards of fabric for backing
73" x 89" piece of batting

Cutting the Layered Pieces

Refer to "Rotary Cutting" on page 6 to stack the fabrics on top of each other and straighten the edges. Refer to the cutting diagram below to cut the layered fabrics into the following pieces, cutting in order from left to right.

From *each* of the ⅝-yard cuts of fabric for blocks, cut:
16 squares, 5½" x 5½" (80 total)
4 squares, 2" x 2" (20 total)

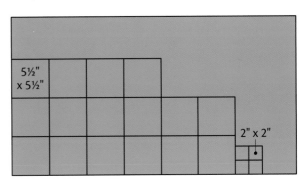

Cutting the Remaining Pieces

From the white tone-on-tone print, cut:
12 strips, 2" x 42"; crosscut into 80 rectangles, 2" x 5½"
3 squares, 17½" x 17½"; cut twice diagonally to yield 12 side setting triangles (you will use 10)
2 squares, 9" x 9"; cut once diagonally to yield 4 corner setting triangles

From the fabric for inner border, cut:
8 strips, 2½" x 42"

From the fabric for outer border and binding, cut:
8 strips, 6½" x 42"
8 strips, 2½" x 42"

Designed by Kathy Brown; pieced by Linda Reed; quilted by Carol Hilton

Constructing the Blocks

1. Organize the layered block pieces into stacks, separating them first by fabric and then by size. Label the fabrics 1–5. Also make a stack from the white rectangles.

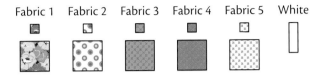

Fabric 1 Fabric 2 Fabric 3 Fabric 4 Fabric 5 White

2. To make block A, arrange one 5½" square each of fabrics 1–4, four tone-on-tone print 2" x 5½" rectangles, and one 2" square of fabric 5 into three horizontal rows as shown. Sew the pieces in each row together. Press the seam allowances toward the squares. Sew the rows together. Press the seam allowances away from the center row. Repeat to make a total of four blocks.

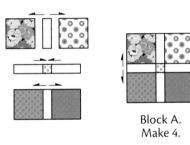

Block A.
Make 4.

3. Repeat step 2 with the remaining squares and rectangles in the combinations shown to make blocks B–E. Make four of each block.

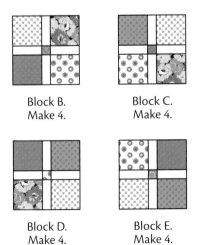

Block B.
Make 4.

Block C.
Make 4.

Block D.
Make 4.

Block E.
Make 4.

Assembling the Quilt Top

1. Set aside one D and one E block for another project. Refer to the quilt assembly diagram to arrange the remaining blocks and the side setting triangles into six diagonal rows, using a design wall or other flat surface. Position the corner triangles at each corner.

2. Sew the blocks and side setting triangles in each row together. Press as shown. Sew the rows together. Press the seam allowances in one direction. Add the corner setting triangles last. Press the seam allowances away from the triangles.

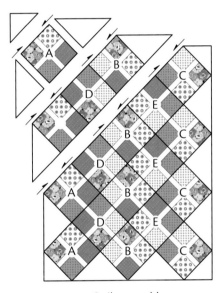

Quilt assembly

Adding the Borders

1. Referring to "Adding Borders" on page 7, join two 2½" x 42" inner-border strips end to end to make one long strip. Repeat to make a total of four pieced strips. Sew the border strips to the quilt top. Press.

2. Repeat step 1 to add the 6½" x 42" outer-border strips to the quilt top.

Finishing

Refer to "Completing the Quilt" on page 7 to layer the quilt top, batting, and backing. Quilt as desired. Bind the quilt with the 2½"-wide binding strips.

Designed by Kathy Brown; pieced by Linda Reed; quilted by Sandra Guilbeau

Take 5... Across the Miles

The blending of neutral prints with a brown checked fabric creates this softly romantic Irish Chain bed quilt.

Finished Quilt: 88" x 112"
Finished Block: 12" x 12"

Materials

Yardage is based on 42"-wide fabric.
1½ yards of tan print A for blocks
1½ yards of tan print B for blocks
1½ yards of tan print C for blocks
1½ yards of tan striped fabric for blocks*
2⅛ yards of brown checked fabric for blocks and inner border
2½ yards of one of the tan block fabrics for outer border and binding
8 yards of fabric for backing
100" x 124" piece of batting

The stripe should run the length of the fabric.

Cutting the Layered Pieces

Refer to "Rotary Cutting" on page 6 to stack the fabrics on top of each other and straighten the edges. Refer to the cutting diagram below to cut the layered fabrics into the following pieces, cutting pieces of the same size in order from left to right.

From *each* of the 1½-yard cuts of fabric for blocks, cut:
24 squares, 6½" x 6½" (96 total)
48 squares, 2½" x 2½" (192 total)
48 rectangles, 2½" x 4½" (192 total)

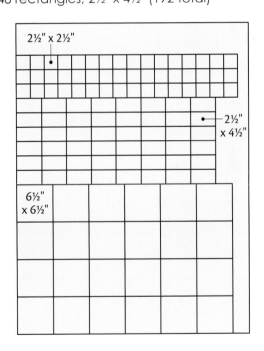

Cutting the Remaining Pieces

From the brown checked fabric, cut:
28 strips, 2½" x 42"; crosscut 18 strips into 288 squares, 2½" x 2½"

From the fabric for outer border and binding, cut:
12 strips, 6½" x 42"
11 strips, 2¾" x 42"

Constructing the Blocks

1. Organize the layered block pieces and the brown checked squares into stacks, separating them first by fabric and then by size. Label the fabrics 1–5, with the brown checked squares as fabric 5.

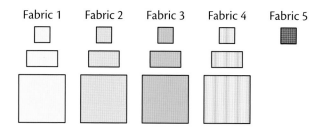

2. To make block A, arrange two fabric 1 rectangles, two 2½" fabric 1 squares, and three fabric 5 squares into three horizontal rows. Sew the pieces in each row together. Press the seam allowances toward fabric 5. Sew the rows together. Press the seam allowances away from the middle row. Repeat to make a total of 24 units.

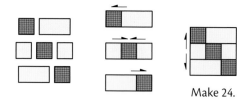

Make 24.

3. Sew a 6½" fabric 1 square to the right edge of a unit from step 2, making sure the brown checked squares are oriented correctly. Press the seam allowances toward the fabric 1 square. Repeat to make a total of 24 units.

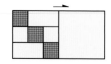

Make 24.

4. Sew two units from step 3 together to complete the block. Repeat to make a total of 12 blocks.

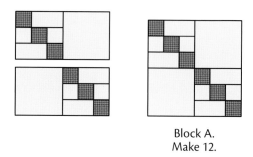

Block A.
Make 12.

5. Repeat steps 2–4 with the remaining squares and rectangles in the combinations shown to make blocks B–D and D reversed. Make 12 each of blocks B and C and 6 each of D and D reversed, being sure to orient the stripes correctly in the D and D reversed blocks.

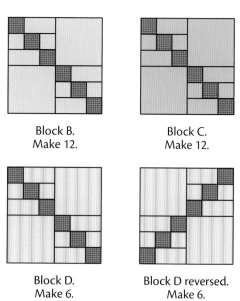

Block B.
Make 12.

Block C.
Make 12.

Block D.
Make 6.

Block D reversed.
Make 6.

Assembling the Quilt Top

1. Refer to the quilt assembly diagram on page 33 to arrange the blocks into eight rows of six blocks each, using a design wall or other flat surface.

2. Sew the blocks in each row together. Press the seam allowances in opposite directions from row to row. Sew the rows together. Press the seam allowances in one direction.

Adding the Borders

1. Referring to "Adding Borders" on page 7, join three 2½" x 42" inner-border strips end to end to make one long strip. Repeat to make a total of two pieced strips. Add these borders to the sides of the quilt top. Press. Sew the remaining strips into pairs end to end to make two long strips. Sew these strips to the top and bottom edges of the quilt top. Press.

2. Join three 6½" x 42" outer-border strips end to end to make one long strip. Repeat to make a total of four pieced strips. Sew the strips to the quilt top in the same manner as for the inner border.

Finishing

Refer to "Completing the Quilt" on page 7 to layer the quilt top, batting, and backing. Quilt as desired. Bind the quilt with the 2¾"-wide binding strips.

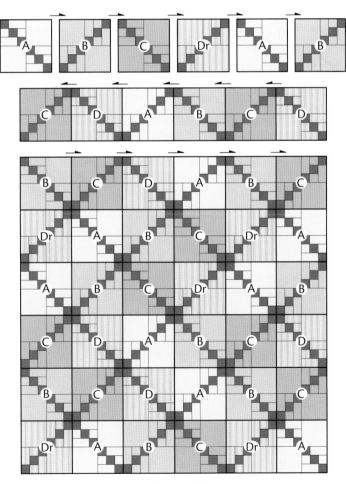

Quilt assembly

Designed by Kathy Brown; pieced by Linda Reed; quilted by Sandra Guilbeau

Take 5...Knows Variety Is the Spice of Life

Children of all ages, including those with special needs, benefit from the sensory experiences gained through exploring simple shapes with various textures. Chenille, cotton, corduroy, synthetic micro plush (such as Minkee), and flannel work together to provide visual and tactile stimulation in this ever-so-easy quilt.

Finished Quilt: 36" x 42"
Finished Block: 6" x 6"

Materials

Yardage is based on 42"-wide fabric.
¼ yard of yellow flannel for blocks
¼ yard of green checked micro plush for blocks
¼ yard of purple cotton print for blocks
¼ yard of pink corduroy for blocks
¼ yard of striped chenille for blocks
⅓ yard of one of the block fabrics for inner border
⅝ yard of one of the block fabrics for outer border
½ yard of purple print for binding
2½ yards of fabric for backing
44" x 50" piece of batting

Cutting the Layered Pieces

Refer to "Rotary Cutting" on page 6 to stack the fabrics on top of each other and straighten the edges. Refer to the cutting diagram below to cut the layered fabrics into the following pieces, cutting in order from left to right.

From each of the ¼-yard cuts of fabric for blocks, cut:
4 squares, 6½" x 6½" (20 total)

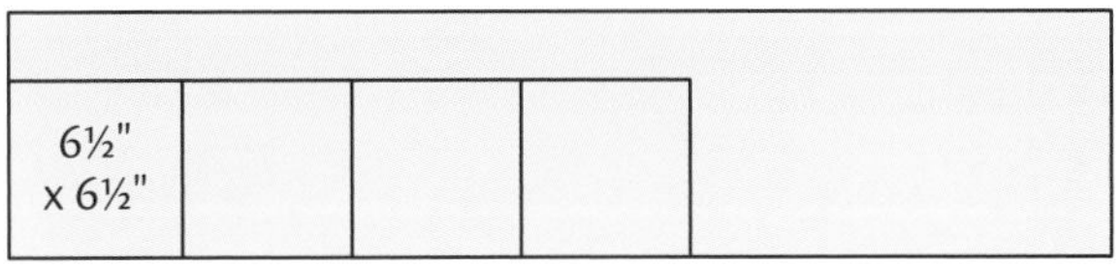

6½" x 6½"

Cutting the Remaining Pieces

From the fabric for inner border, cut:
4 strips, 2½" x 42"

From the fabric for outer border, cut:
4 strips, 4½" x 42"

From the purple print, cut:
5 strips, 2½" x 42"

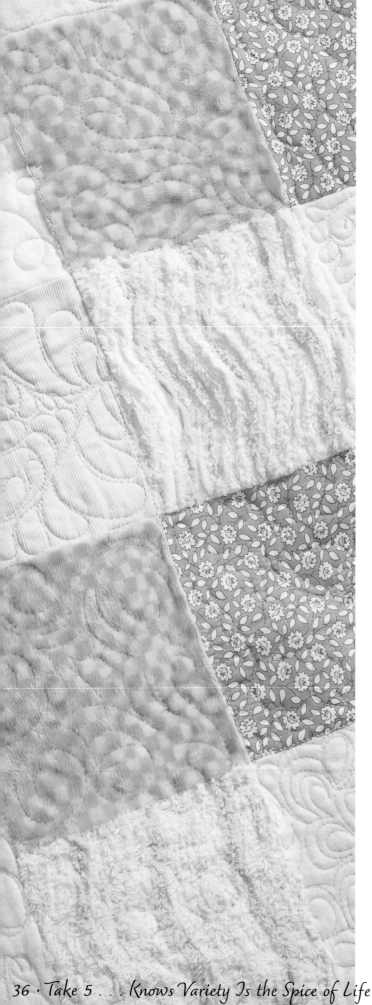

Assembling the Quilt Top

1. Separate the layered block pieces into stacks by fabric. Label the fabrics 1–5.

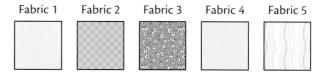

Fabric 1   Fabric 2   Fabric 3   Fabric 4   Fabric 5

2. Refer to the quilt assembly diagram to arrange the 6½" squares into five rows of four squares each, using a design wall or other flat surface.
3. Sew the blocks in each row together. Press the seam allowances open. Sew the rows together. Press the seam allowances open.

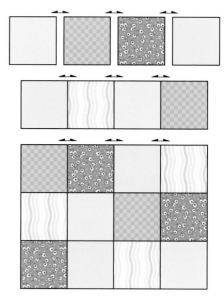

Quilt assembly

Adding the Borders

1. Referring to "Adding Borders" on page 7, sew the 2½" x 42" inner-border strips to the quilt top. Press.
2. Repeat step 1 to add the 4½" x 42" outer-border strips to the quilt top.

Finishing

Refer to "Completing the Quilt" on page 7 to layer the quilt top, batting, and backing. Quilt as desired. Bind the quilt with the purple print 2½"-wide strips.

Take 5... Loves an Autograph Hound

Create a wonderful remembrance of a special occasion with a Take 5 autograph quilt. Change the fabrics to fit the event, and this quilt will be suited for the young and the young at heart alike.

Finished Quilt: 50" x 58½"
Finished Block: 6" x 6"

Materials

Yardage is based on 42"-wide fabric.
⅓ yard of black print for blocks
⅓ yard of red print for blocks
⅓ yard of green print for blocks
⅓ yard of tan print for blocks
1 yard of muslin for blocks and setting triangles
½ yard of one of the block prints for inner border
2⅛ yards of one of the block prints for outer border and binding
3¼ yards of fabric for backing
58" x 67" piece of batting

Cutting the Layered Pieces

Refer to "Rotary Cutting" on page 6 to stack the fabrics on top of each other and straighten the edges. Refer to the cutting diagram below to cut the layered fabrics into the following pieces, cutting in order from left to right.

From each of the ⅓-yard cuts of fabric for blocks, cut:
16 rectangles, 2½" x 6½" (64 total)

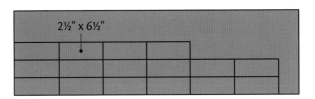

Cutting the Remaining Pieces

From the muslin, cut:
6 strips, 2½" x 42"; crosscut into 32 rectangles, 2½" x 6½"
4 squares, 9¾" x 9¾"; cut twice diagonally to yield 16 side setting triangles (you will use 14)
2 squares, 5⅛" x 5⅛"; cut once diagonally to yield 4 corner setting triangles

From the fabric for inner border, cut:
6 strips, 2½" x 42"

From the fabric for outer border and binding, cut:
8 strips, 6½" x 42"
6 strips, 2½" x 42"

Designed by Kathy Brown; pieced by Linda Reed; quilted by Carol Hilton

Constructing the Blocks

1. Separate the layered block pieces into stacks by fabric. Label the fabrics 1–4. Also make a stack of the muslin rectangles.

2. To make block A, sew a fabric 1 rectangle to each long edge of a muslin rectangle. Press the seam allowances toward fabric 1. Repeat to make a total of eight blocks.

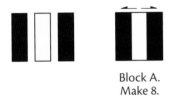

Block A.
Make 8.

3. Repeat step 2 with the remaining rectangles in the combinations shown to make blocks B–D. Make eight of each block.

Block B.
Make 8.

Block C.
Make 8.

Block D.
Make 8.

Assembling the Quilt Top

1. Refer to the quilt assembly diagram to arrange the blocks and the side setting triangles into eight diagonal rows, using a design wall or other flat surface. Position the corner triangles at each corner.

2. Sew the blocks and side setting triangles in each row together. Press as shown. Sew the rows together. Press the seam allowances in one direction. Add the corner setting triangles last. Press the seam allowances away from the triangles.

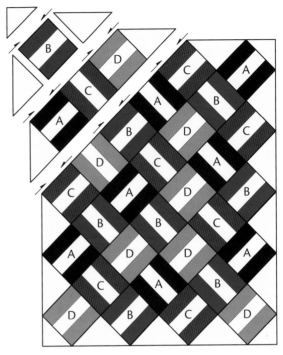

Quilt assembly

Adding the Borders

1. Referring to "Adding Borders" on page 7, join two 2½" x 42" inner-border strips end to end to make one long strip. Repeat to make a total of two pieced strips. Sew the border strips to the sides of the quilt top. Press. Sew the remaining two inner-border strips to the top and bottom edges of the quilt top. Press.

2. Join two 6½" x 42" outer-border strips end to end to make one long strip. Repeat to make a total of four pieced strips. Sew the border strips to the quilt top. Press.

Finishing

Refer to "Completing the Quilt" on page 7 to layer the quilt top, batting, and backing. Quilt as desired. Bind the quilt with the 2½"-wide binding strips.

Color It Bright!

Cheerful primary-colored fabrics make this version of "Take 5...Loves an Autograph Hound" (page 37) perfect for a youngster's birthday party or end-of-the-school-year celebration.

Designed and pieced by Kathy Brown; quilted by Ellen Rushin

Take 5...Rides the Rails

A simple Rail Fence explores its scrappy side in this inviting version of a Take 5 quilt!

Finished Quilt: 66" x 76"
Finished Block: 10" x 10"

Materials

Yardage is based on 42"-wide fabric.

⅔ yard of black print for blocks
⅔ yard of multicolored paisley for blocks
⅔ yard of green print for blocks
⅔ yard of red print for blocks
⅔ yard of tan solid for blocks
⅔ yard of one of the block prints for inner
 border
2¼ yards of one of the block prints for outer
 border and binding
4⅝ yards of fabric for backing
74" x 84" piece of batting

Cutting the Layered Pieces

Refer to ìRotary Cuttingî on page 6 to stack the fabrics on top of each other and straighten the edges. Refer to the cutting diagram below to cut the layered fabrics into the following pieces, cutting in order from left to right.

From each of the ⅔-yard cuts of fabric for blocks, cut:

30 rectangles, 2½" x 10½" (150 total)

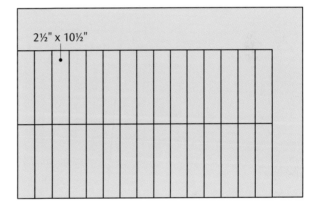

2½" x 10½"

Cutting the Remaining Pieces

From the fabric for inner border, cut:
8 strips, 2½" x 42"

From the fabric for outer border and binding, cut:
8 strips, 6½" x 42"
8 strips, 2½" x 42"

Designed by Kathy Brown; pieced by Linda Reed;
quilted by Sandra Guilbeau and Jamie Wallen

Constructing the Blocks

1. Separate the layered block pieces into stacks by fabric. Label the fabrics 1–5.

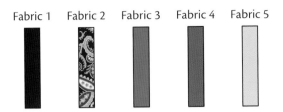

2. To make block A, arrange one rectangle of each fabric in the order shown. Sew the rectangles together along the long edges. Repeat to make a total of six blocks.

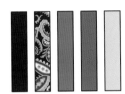

Block A.
Make 6.

3. Repeat step 2 with the remaining rectangles, arranging them in the order shown for each block. Make six of each block.

Block B.
Make 6.

Block C.
Make 6.

Block D.
Make 6.

Block E.
Make 6.

Assembling the Quilt Top

1. Refer to the quilt assembly diagram to arrange the blocks into six rows of five blocks each, using a design wall or other flat surface.
2. Sew the blocks in each row together. Press the seam allowances in opposite directions from row to row. Sew the rows together. Press the seam allowances in one direction.

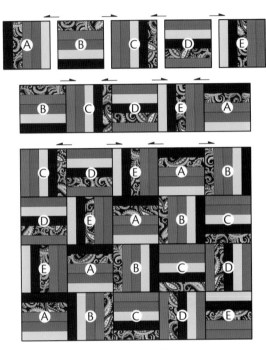

Quilt assembly

Adding the Borders

1. Referring to "Adding Borders" on page 7, join two 2½" x 42" inner-border strips end to end to make one long strip. Repeat to make a total of four pieced strips. Sew the border strips to the quilt top. Press.
2. Repeat step 1 to add the 6½" x 42" outer-border strips to the quilt top.

Finishing

Refer to "Completing the Quilt" on page 7 to layer the quilt top, batting, and backing. Quilt as desired. Bind the quilt with the 2½"-wide binding strips.

Designed by Kathy Brown; pieced by Linda Reed; quilted by Carol Hilton

Take 5... Comes Home for the Holidays

Comfy and cozy, this scrappy Log Cabin quilt is sure to become a holiday favorite in your heart and home.

Finished Quilt: 72" x 86"
Finished Block: 14" x 14"

Materials

Yardage is based on 42"-wide fabric.
1⅛ yards of light tan print for blocks
1⅛ yards of black print for blocks
1⅛ yards of rusty red print for blocks
1⅛ yards of dark green print for blocks
1⅛ yards of deep gold print for blocks
⅔ yard of one of the block prints for inner border
2⅓ yards of one of the block prints for outer border and binding
5¼ yards of fabric for backing
80" x 94" piece of batting

Cutting the Layered Pieces

Refer to "Rotary Cutting" on page 6 to stack the fabrics on top of each other and straighten the edges. Refer to the cutting diagram at right to cut the layered fabrics into the following pieces, cutting pieces of the same size in order from left to right.

From *each* of the 1⅛-yard cuts of fabric for blocks, cut:

4 squares, 2½" x 2½" (20 total)
4 rectangles, 2" x 3" (A) (20 total)
8 rectangles, 2" x 5" (B) (40 total)
8 rectangles, 2" x 6" (C) (40 total)
8 rectangles, 2" x 8" (D) (40 total)
8 rectangles, 2" x 9" (E) (40 total)
8 rectangles, 2" x 11" (F) (40 total)
8 rectangles, 2" x 12" (G) (40 total)
8 rectangles, 2" x 14" (H) (40 total)
4 rectangles, 2" x 15" (I) (20 total)

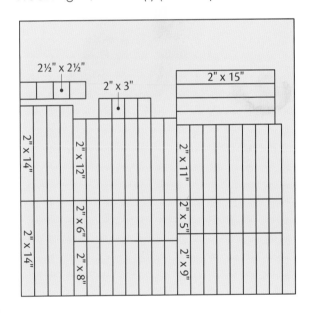

Cutting the Remaining Pieces

From the fabric for inner border, cut:
8 strips, 2½" x 42"

From the fabric for outer border and binding, cut:
8 strips, 6½" x 42"
9 strips, 2½" x 42"

Constructing the Blocks

1. Organize the layered block pieces into stacks, separating them first by fabric and then by size. Label the fabrics 1–5 and arrange the rectangles in order from shortest to longest.

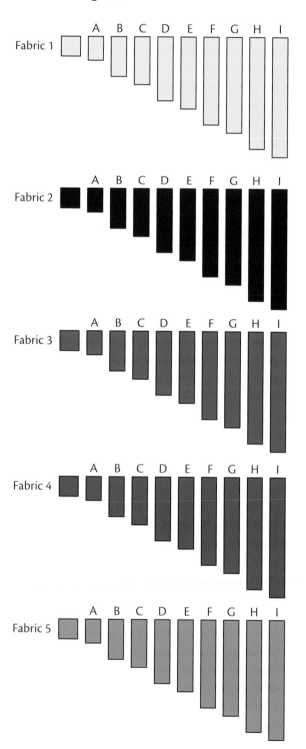

2. To make block A, sew an A rectangle of fabric 2 to the right edge of a fabric 1 square, aligning the end of the strip with the bottom of the square. Press the seam allowance away from the square. Trim the excess even with the top of the square. Sew a B rectangle of fabric 2 to the top of the previous unit. Press and trim the excess as before. Add a B rectangle of fabric 3 to the left edge of the unit; press and trim as before. Working counterclockwise in the established pattern, continue adding rectangles to the unit in the order shown for a total of four rounds, pressing and trimming after each addition. Repeat to make a total of four blocks.

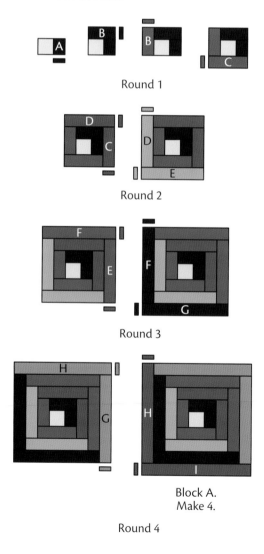

Round 1

Round 2

Round 3

Block A.
Make 4.

Round 4

3. Repeat step 2 with the remaining squares and rectangles in the combinations shown to make blocks B–E. Make four of each block.

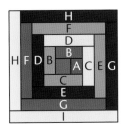

Block B.
Make 4.

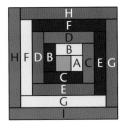

Block C.
Make 4.

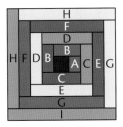

Block D.
Make 4.

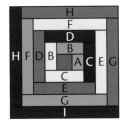

Block E.
Make 4.

Assembling the Quilt Top

1. Refer to the quilt assembly diagram to arrange the blocks into five rows of four blocks each, using a design wall or other flat surface.
2. Sew the blocks in each row together. Press the seam allowances in opposite directions from row to row. Sew the rows together. Press the seam allowances in one direction.

Quilt assembly

Adding the Borders

1. Referring to "Adding Borders" on page 7, join two 2½" x 42" inner-border strips end to end to make one long strip. Repeat to make a total of four strips. Sew the border strips to the quilt top.
2. Repeat step 1 to add the 6½" x 42" outer-border strips to the quilt top.

Finishing

Refer to "Completing the Quilt" on page 7 to layer the quilt top, batting, and backing. Quilt as desired. Bind the quilt with the 2½"-wide binding strips.

Designed by Kathy Brown; pieced by Linda Reed; quilted by Carol Hilton

Take 5... Makes Mud Pies

Shades of brown and cream evoke childhood memories of making mud pies in this Snow-ball version of a Take 5 quilt.

Finished Quilt: 61" x 79"
Finished Block: 9" x 9"

Materials

Yardage is based on 42"-wide fabric.
1 yard of cream marbled fabric for blocks
1 yard of light brown marbled fabric for blocks
1 yard of medium brown marbled fabric for blocks
1 yard of very dark brown marbled fabric for blocks
1 yard of dark brown marbled fabric for blocks
⅔ yard of one of the block prints for inner border
2¼ yards of one of the block prints for outer border and binding
4⅞ yards of fabric for backing
69" x 87" piece of batting

Cutting the Layered Pieces

Refer to "Rotary Cutting" on page 6 to stack the fabrics on top of each other and straighten the edges. Refer to the cutting diagram below to cut the layered fabrics into the following pieces, cutting pieces of the same size in order from left to right.

From *each* of the 1-yard cuts of fabric for blocks, cut:
7 squares, 9½" x 9½" (35 total)
28 squares, 3½" x 3½" (140 total)

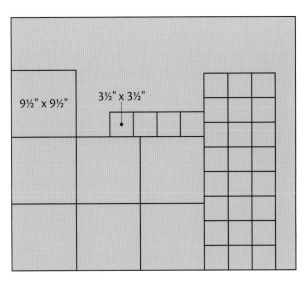

Cutting the Remaining Pieces

From the fabric for inner border, cut:
8 strips, 2½" x 42"

From the fabric for outer border and binding, cut:
8 strips, 6½" x 42"
8 strips, 2½" x 42"

Constructing the Blocks

1. Organize the layered block pieces into stacks, separating them first by fabric and then by size. Label the fabrics 1–5.

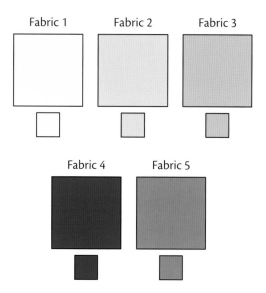

2. With a fabric-marking pencil, draw a diagonal line from corner to corner on the wrong side of each 3½" square.

3. To make block A, with right sides together and raw edges aligned, position a marked square of fabric 2 on the upper-left corner of a 9½" square of fabric 1, orienting the marked line as shown. Sew on the marked line. Trim ¼" from the stitching line. Press the resulting triangle toward the corner. Repeat on the remaining three corners, orienting the marked lines as shown. Repeat to make a total of seven blocks.

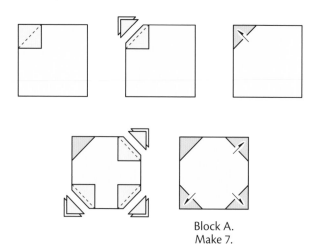

Block A.
Make 7.

4. Repeat step 3 with the remaining squares in the combinations shown to make blocks B–E. Make seven of each block.

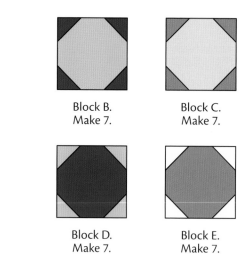

Block B.
Make 7.

Block C.
Make 7.

Block D.
Make 7.

Block E.
Make 7.

Assembling the Quilt Top

1. Refer to the quilt assembly diagram to arrange the blocks into seven rows of five blocks each, using a design wall or other flat surface.

2. Sew the blocks in each row together. Press the seam allowances in opposite directions from row to row. Sew the rows together. Press the seam allowances in one direction.

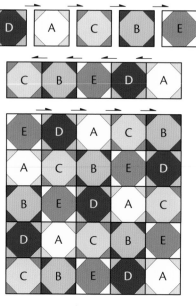

Quilt assembly

Adding the Borders

1. Referring to "Adding Borders" on page 7, join two 2½" x 42" inner-border strips end to end to make one long strip. Repeat to make a total of four pieced strips. Sew the border strips to the quilt top. Press.
2. Repeat step 1 to add the 6½" x 42" outer-border strips to the quilt top.

Finishing

Refer to "Completing the Quilt" on page 7 to layer the quilt top, batting, and backing. Quilt as desired. Bind the quilt with the 2½"-wide binding strips.

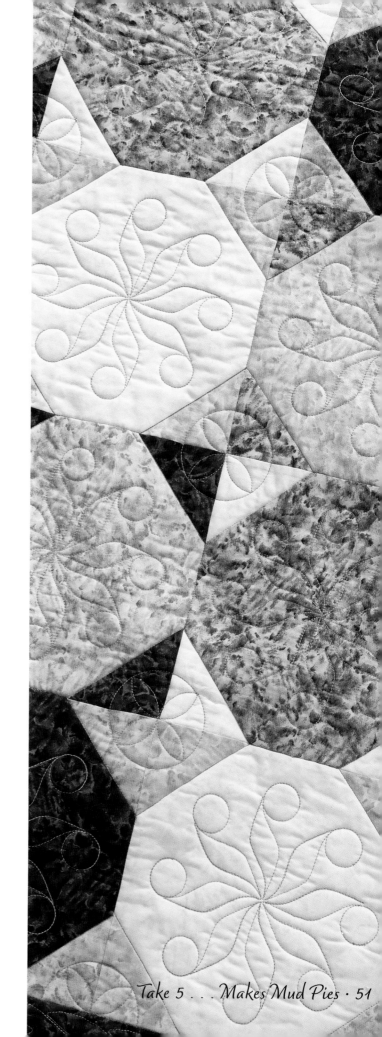

Designed and pieced by Kathy Brown; quilted by Rachel Justus

Take 5... Deserves an Even Break

Can you find the broken stars hiding among the blocks?

Finished Quilt: 61" x 79"
Finished Block: 9" x 9"

Materials

Yardage is based on 42"-wide fabric.

1 yard of cream floral for blocks
1 yard of sage green print for blocks
1 yard of vintage blue ticking stripe for blocks
1 yard of vintage plum floral for blocks
1 yard of rose print for blocks
⅔ yard of one of the block prints for inner border
2¼ yards of one of the block prints for outer border and binding
4⅞ yards of fabric for backing
69" x 87" piece of batting

Cutting the Layered Pieces

Refer to "Rotary Cutting" on page 6 to stack the fabrics on top of each other and straighten the edges. Refer to the cutting diagram below to cut the layered fabrics into the following pieces, cutting in order from left to right.

From *each* of the 1-yard cuts of fabric for blocks, cut:
7 squares, 9½" x 9½" (35 total)
14 squares, 4" x 4" (70 total)

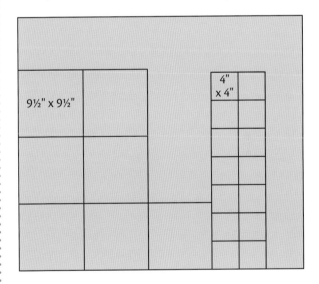

Cutting the Remaining Pieces

From the fabric for inner border, cut:
8 strips, 2½" x 42"

From the fabric for outer border and binding, cut:
8 strips, 6½" x 42"
8 strips, 2½" x 42"

Constructing the Blocks

1. Organize the layered block pieces into stacks, separating them first by fabric and then by size. Label the fabrics 1–5.

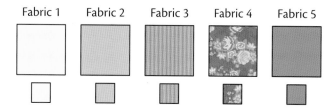

2. With a fabric-marking pencil, draw a diagonal line from corner to corner on the wrong side of each 4" square.

3. To make block A, with right sides together and raw edges aligned, place a marked square of fabric 2 on the upper-left corner of a 9½" square of fabric 1, orienting the marked line as shown. Sew on the marked line. Trim ¼" from the stitching line. Press the resulting triangle toward the corner. Sew a marked square of fabric 3 to the lower-right corner in the same manner.

Block A.
Make 7.

4. Repeat step 3 with the remaining squares in the combinations shown to make blocks B–E. Make seven of each block.

Block B.
Make 7.

Block C.
Make 7.

Block D.
Make 7.

Block E.
Make 7.

Assembling the Quilt Top

1. Refer to the quilt assembly diagram to arrange the blocks into seven rows of five blocks each, using a design wall or other flat surface.

2. Sew the blocks in each row together. Press the seam allowances in opposite directions from row to row. Sew the rows together. Press the seam allowances in one direction.

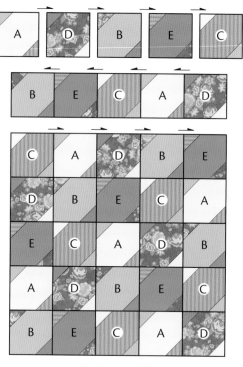

Quilt assembly

Adding the Borders

1. Referring to "Adding Borders" on page 7, join two 2½" x 42" inner-border strips end to end to make one long strip. Repeat to make a total of four pieced strips. Sew the border strips to the quilt top. Press.

2. Repeat step 1 to add the 6½" x 42" outer-border strips to the quilt top.

Finishing

Refer to "Completing the Quilt" on page 7 to layer the quilt top, batting, and backing. Quilt as desired. Bind the quilt with the 2½"-wide binding strips.

Take 5...Has Yo-Yos to Go-Go

Liven up plain squares by placing festive yo-yos at the block intersections.

Finished Quilt: 61" x 79"
Finished Block: 9" x 9"

Materials

Yardage is based on 42"-wide fabric.
1 yard of brick red print for blocks
1 yard of mustard print for blocks
1 yard of olive print for blocks
1 yard of tan print for blocks
1 yard of black print for blocks
⅔ yard of one of the block prints for inner border
2¼ yards of one of the block prints for outer border and binding
4⅞ yards of fabric for backing
69" x 87" piece of batting
24 black 1"-diameter buttons (optional)

Cutting the Layered Pieces

Refer to "Rotary Cutting" on page 6 to stack the fabrics on top of each other and straighten the edges. Refer to the cutting diagram below to cut the layered fabrics into the following pieces, cutting in order from left to right.

From *each* of the 1-yard cuts of fabric for blocks, cut:

12 squares, 9½" x 9½" (60 total)

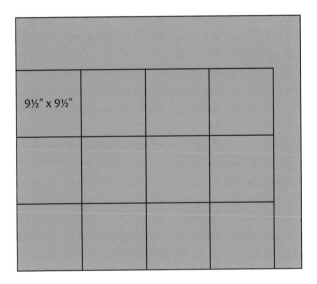

Cutting the Remaining Pieces

From the fabric for inner border, cut:

8 strips, 2½" x 42"

From the fabric for outer border and binding, cut:

8 strips, 6½" x 42"
8 strips, 2½" x 42"

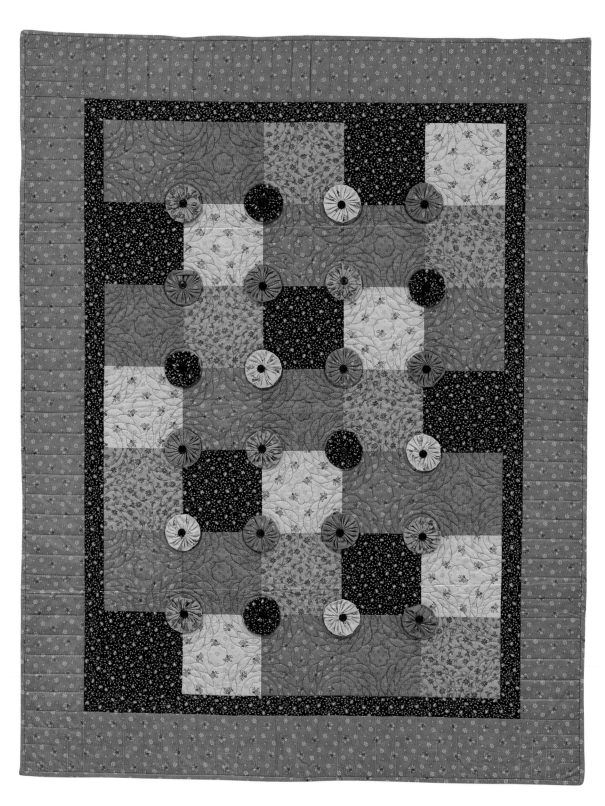

Designed and pieced by Kathy Brown; quilted by Carol Hilton

Assembling the Quilt Top

1. Separate the layered block pieces into stacks by fabric. Label the fabrics 1–5.

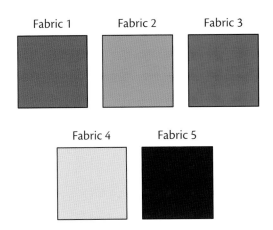

Fabric 1   Fabric 2   Fabric 3

Fabric 4   Fabric 5

2. Refer to the quilt assembly diagram to arrange the 9½" squares into seven rows of five squares each, using a design wall or other flat surface.
3. Sew the blocks in each row together. Press the seam allowances in opposite directions from row to row. Sew the rows together. Press the seam allowances in one direction.

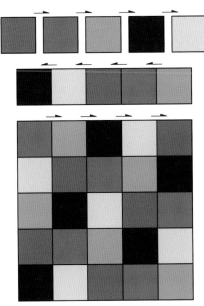

Quilt assembly

Adding the Borders

1. Referring to "Adding Borders" on page 7, join two 2½" x 42" inner-border strips end to end to make one long strip. Repeat to make a total of four pieced strips. Sew the border strips to the quilt top. Press.
2. Repeat step 1 with the 6½" x 42" outer-border strips.

Finishing

1. Refer to "Completing the Quilt" on page 7 to layer the quilt top, batting, and backing. Quilt as desired. Bind the quilt with the 2½"-wide binding strips.
2. To make the yo-yos, draw a 9½"-diameter circle on the wrong side of each of the remaining 9½" squares. Cut out each circle. Thread a hand-sewing needle with a single strand of strong thread long enough to go around the circle with some to spare. Fold under a ¼" hem to the wrong side around the circumference of one of the circles and baste it in place, leaving a thread tail at each end. Once you've stitched around the entire perimeter of the fabric circle, gently pull the ends of your stitching thread to gather the yo-yo edges toward the center. Make a couple of stitches to secure your gathers, and then knot the ends and trim your thread. Repeat with the remaining fabric circles.

3. Refer to the photo on page 56 to hand tack a yo-yo to the quilt top at each point where four squares intersect, taking a stitch at several points around the edge of each yo-yo with matching thread. You will have one yo-yo left over; set it aside for another project or add it to your label. Stitch a button to the center of each yo-yo, if desired, for added fun!

Table topper.
Designed and quilted by Kathy Brown; pieced by Linda Reed.

Take 5... For the Table

Take 5 does double duty as a table topper and table runner (shown on page 61) duo! Although fantastic in reproduction fabrics, this easy-to-make pair would look fantastic in holiday-themed fabrics for special occasions as well. Blocks for both pieces are made at the same time so you'll be finished with two projects in a snap.

Finished Table Topper: 44" x 44"
Finished Table Runner: 17" x 44"
Finished Block: 9" x 9"

Materials (for table topper and runner)

Yardage is based on 42"-wide fabric.
⅝ yard of brown paisley print for blocks
⅝ yard of brown mottled print for blocks
⅝ yard of turquoise print for blocks
⅝ yard of white-with-turquoise print for blocks
⅝ yard of brick red print for blocks
½ yard of one of the block fabrics for inner borders
2 yards of one of the block fabrics for outer borders and bindings
4 yards of fabric for backings
4 yards of batting

Cutting the Layered Pieces

Refer to "Rotary Cutting" on page 6 to stack the fabrics on top of each other and straighten the edges. Refer to the cutting diagram below to cut the layered fabrics into the following pieces, cutting in order from left to right.

From each of the ⅝-yard cuts of fabric for blocks, cut:
4 squares, 6½" x 6½" (20 total)
16 squares, 3½" x 3½" (70 total; you will use 68)
4 rectangles, 3½" x 6½" (20 total)

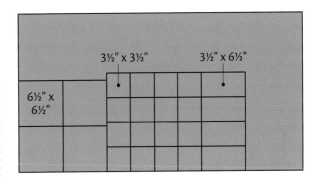

Cutting the Remaining Pieces

From the fabric for inner borders, cut:
7 strips, 1½" x 42"; crosscut into:
    4 strips, 1½" x 36½"
    2 strips, 1½" x 38½"
    2 strips, 1½" x 10½"

From the fabric for outer borders and binding, cut:
7 strips, 3½" x 42"; crosscut into:
    6 strips, 3½" x 38½"
    2 strips, 3½" x 10½"
8 strips, 2½" x 42"

Constructing the Blocks

1. Separate the layered block pieces into stacks by fabric. Label the fabrics 1–5.

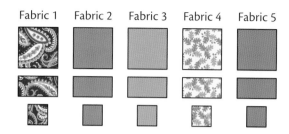

Fabric 1   Fabric 2   Fabric 3   Fabric 4   Fabric 5

2. To make block A, sew a 3½" square of fabric 4 to one side of a 3½" square of fabric 5. Press the seam allowances toward the darker fabric. Sew this unit to the bottom of a 6½" square of fabric 1. Press the seam allowances toward the fabric 1 square. Sew a 3½" square of fabric 3 to the end of a fabric 2 rectangle. Press the seam allowances toward the darker fabric. Add this unit to the right edge of the previous unit. Repeat to make a total of four blocks.

Block A.
Make 4.

3. Repeat step 2 with the remaining squares and rectangles in the combinations shown to make blocks B–E. Make four of each block. The extra 3½" squares will be used in the outer borders.

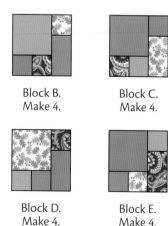

Block B.   Block C.
Make 4.   Make 4.

Block D.   Block E.
Make 4.   Make 4.

Assembling the Table-Runner and Table-Topper Tops

1. For the table runner, arrange four different blocks into one horizontal row. Sew the blocks together. Press the seam allowances in one direction.

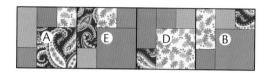

Table-runner assembly

2. For the table topper, referring to the photo on page 58 and the assembly diagram as needed, arrange the remaining 16 blocks into 4 rows of 4 blocks each as desired, rotating the blocks until you're satisfied with the arrangement. Sew the blocks in each row together. Press the seam allowances in opposite directions from row to row. Sew the rows together. Press the seam allowances in one direction.

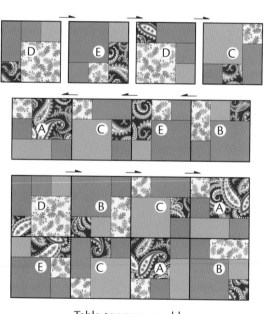

Table-topper assembly

Adding the Borders

1. For the table runner, sew a 1½" x 36½" inner-border strip to each long side of the runner top. Press the seam allowances toward the border strips. Sew the 1½" x 10½" inner-border strips to the short sides of the runner top. Press the seam allowances toward the border strips.

2. Sew a 3½" x 38½" outer-border strip to each long side of the runner top. Press the seam allowances toward the outer-border strips. Select four matching 3½" squares and sew one to each end of the two 3½" x 10½" strips. Press the seam allowances toward the border strips. Add these strips to the short sides of the runner top. Press the seam allowances toward the outer-border strips.

3. For the table topper, sew the remaining 1½" x 36½" inner-border strips to the sides of the table-topper top. Press the seam allowances toward the borders. Sew the 1½" x 38½" inner-border strips to the top and bottom edges of the table topper top. Press the seam allowances toward the borders.

4. Add 3½" x 38½" outer-border strips to the sides of the table topper. Press the seam allowances toward the outer-border strips. Select four matching 3½" squares of fabric and sew one to each end of the remaining 3½" x 38½" outer-border strips. Press the seam allowances toward the border strips. Sew these strips to the top and bottom edges of the topper. Press the seam allowances toward the outer-border strips.

Finishing

Refer to "Completing the Quilt" on page 7 to layer the quilt top, and table runner each with batting and backing. Quilt each piece as desired. Bind each piece with the 2½"-wide binding strips.

Table runner

Acknowledgments

With a grateful heart, I give warm thanks to:

- My husband, Michael, who keeps our household centered and grounded. Your talent and green thumb have created the peaceful oasis that is our backyard, giving me a place that allows me to escape the hectic pace I create for myself. I appreciate your love, your never-ending abundance of encouragement, and your ability to bring a calm wind in the face of a raging storm.

- Erin, the most wonderful daughter any mother could ever hope to have. You are an inspiration to me, and I admire your tenacity, determination, generosity, and kindness. But most of all, I appreciate your loving and caring heart. ILYBTTWS!

- My mom, who knew that her tomboy would eventually grow into a daughter and gave me the patience and the tools to see it through.

- My dad, who saw my love for color at an early age and fostered it through that box of 120 Crayola crayons he purchased from Shopper's Fair and snuck home.

- Janice Loewenthal, best friend and the sister that I never had. We entered this quilting journey together, and we'll see it through together to the end.

- Linda Reed, a gracious friend and true inspiration. You keep me going even when I think I have nothing left to go on, and then you encourage me to fly even higher. I could not have done this without you.

- Mark Lipinski, a wonderful friend and sounding board, who took me by the hand and helped me make the leap into writing this book. XOXO!

- Sandra Guilbeau and Mynan Guidry of the Quilt Corner in Baton Rouge. You have taught so much and given so much. I treasure our friendship.

- The ladies in the Southern Ladies Quilting Society who are with me every Wednesday, keeping me grounded, giving me encouragement, offering strong shoulders, and letting me escape from my studio for a few precious hours each week.

- Leanne Anderson of the Whole Country Caboodle, who opened her heart 15 years ago and shared a vast wealth of knowledge to a fledgling pattern designer. You'll never know what that meant to me.

- The quilters who helped pull these fabrics together and make beautiful quilts: Linda Reed (whom I never tire of thanking!) and Pam Vierra McGinnis. You transformed my sketches and words into beautiful quilts to treasure, and I treasure your invaluable contribution.

- Sandra Guilbeau, Carol Hilton, Rachel Justis, Ellen Rushin, Karen McTavish, and Jamie Wallen for their excellent machine-quilting skills and for fitting my quilts into their busy schedules.

- Cheryl Wilks, Ann Reily, Janelle Crosslin, and Denise Bayer for hours and hours of hand binding!

- The wonderful, generous folks at Andover, Batik Textiles, Cherrywood Fabrics, Moda, Northcott, RJR, the Quilt Corner, and Troy Corporation for supplying the fabrics used in these quilts.

- The wonderful and enthusiastic quilters all over the world who have supported my business. You have made it possible for me to live my dream of loving my work.

- And last but not least, the entire staff at Martingale & Company for their encouragement and assistance with this endeavor.

Meet the Author

My mother was an accomplished seamstress who made every garment I wore up until I entered middle school. Although she tried her best to bring me into her world, I was just too much of a tomboy and avoided a sewing machine for as long as I could. Upon my graduation from college, my parents presented me with a brand-new sewing machine. My mother in particular thought it was a wonderful gift for a newly married graduating daughter, but this daughter could see no benefit at the time and promptly put the sewing machine away in a closet.

Having a daughter of my own several years later did not change my views about sewing or the use of a sewing machine. While other young mothers were busy smocking dresses and sewing wonderful play clothes and sundresses for their daughters, I was busy painting my daughter's clothes with whimsical images. It wasn't until 1994 that a chance visit to a quilt shop transformed my world. Walking into that shop was like walking into color heaven. Fabric as far as the eye could see and just as many spools of thread to match greeted my eyes. Inspiration struck, and I realized that I could possibly use a sewing machine as a tool to "draw" onto fabric. I began designing appliquéd clothing, and from there, my pattern business began.

To date, I've designed 12 fabric lines for Troy Corporation and self-published more than 125 patterns and seven booklets. I've been a featured contributor in numerous magazines, including *The Quilter, Create and Decorate, Quick and Easy Quilting, McCall's Quick Quilts,* and *Fabric Trends.* I've had the good fortune of seeing my quilts featured on the cover of *The Quilter* and *Mark Lipinski's Quilter's Home.* I create my patterns with both the experienced quilter and the beginner in mind, crafting designs that may look intricate but are actually very simple to construct. An impatient person myself, my projects are designed to be made in a day or a weekend, allowing the quilter instant gratification! When I'm not designing fabric or new quilt patterns, I'm busy teaching and lecturing for quilt guilds and quilt shops across the United States.

There's More Online!

See an array of Kathy Brown's patterns, read her blog, and learn about her workshops and lectures at www.the-teachers-pet.com.

Visit www.martingale-pub.com for great books about quilting, knitting, crochet, and more!